BRITAIN IN WORLD WAR II

THE Blitz

Patricia Kendell

Based on an original text by
Fiona Reynoldson

WAYLAND

BRITAIN IN WORLD WAR II
Titles in this series
THE BLITZ
EVACUATION

Editor: Jason Hook
Original Design: Nick Cannan
Differentiated Design: Raynor Design
Cover Design: Giles Wheeler
Text Consultant: Norah Granger, University of Brighton

Based on an original text *The Home Front – The Blitz*, by Fiona Reynoldson,
published in 1990 by Wayland Publishers Limited

First published in 1998 by Wayland Publishers Limited, 61 Western Road,
Hove, East Sussex BN3 1JD

Find Wayland on the Internet at http://www.wayland.co.uk

British Library Cataloguing in Publication Data
Kendell, Patricia
    The Blitz. – (Britain in World War II)
    1. Blackouts in war – History – 20th century – Juvenile literature
    2. Great Britain – History – Bombardment, 1944-45 – Juvenile literature
    I Title
    940.5'3'0941

ISBN 0 7502 2284 0

Typeset in England by Raynor Design
Printed and bound in Italy by G. Canale & CsPA, Turin

Cover picture: A postman delivering letters to a bombed street in London.

 See page 31 for ways in which you can use this book to
encourage literacy skills.

Acknowledgements
The quotes in this book were taken from the following sources: *Raiders Overhead*
by Barbara Nixon (p.11); Trustees of the Tom Harrisson Mass-Observation
Archive (p.12); *The World is a Wedding*, by Bernard Kops (p.14); Gerald Cole,
London (p.23).

The publishers would like to thank the following for permission to publish their
pictures: ET Archives Limited 29; Getty Images *cover*; Imperial War Museum 7
(bottom), 8, 14 (both), 15, 16, 18 (both), 19, 20 (below), 22, 23, 26, 27 (top); John
Frost 27 (bottom); Peter Newark's Historical and Military Pictures 4, 5, 9 (both),
11 (bottom), 12, 17 (both), 25 (left), 28 (both); Topham Picture Library 7 (top), 10,
11 (top), 13 (bottom), 20 (inset), 21, 24, 25 (right). The artwork on
pages 4 and 22 was supplied by Peter Bull Art Studio.

Contents

The War Begins

▲ An advertisement showing German planes attacking enemy ships.

World War II began in September 1939. British soldiers went to help the French people fight the German army. But in the spring of 1940, Germany defeated France.

British soldiers were brought back to Britain in ships and boats. The soldiers were defeated and very tired. They had to leave all their guns and tanks in France.

The German leader, Adolf Hitler, thought it would be easy to invade Britain. He made an invasion plan called Operation Sealion.

▶ A map of Hitler's plan to invade Britain. The plan was never carried out.

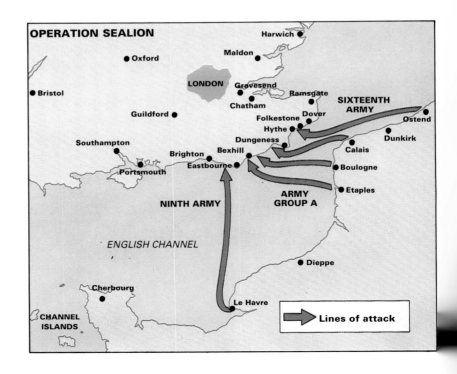

◄ Adolf Hitler was the German leader in World War II.

If Hitler's army tried to sail to Britain, it would be bombed by the British aeroplanes of the Royal Air Force (RAF). So Hitler had to destroy the RAF first.

All through the summer of 1940, German and British aeroplanes fought in the skies. This was called the Battle of Britain.

Both sides lost many aeroplanes, but the RAF was not destroyed. So Hitler thought of another plan. He would bomb London.

———— Preparing for Air Raids ————

People in Britain were expecting to be bombed by the German air force. They thought that thousands of people would be killed or injured. Hospitals were emptied so that there would be room for the wounded. Millions of cardboard coffins were made.

The government thought that German bombs might contain poisonous gas. Everyone was given a gas mask to protect them from this poison.

▶ Gas masks looked like this.

◀ Bags were filled with sand and piled up to protect buildings.

▼ People built their own air-raid shelters.

Shelters and wardens

Public shelters were built to protect people from bombs during air raids. Some people built a shelter in their own garden.

Men and women volunteered to be air-raid wardens. They were given a tin hat, a whistle and a gas mask. The wardens let people into the shelters during an air raid.

Some people came up with funny ideas to protect them from bombs. One person thought a metal umbrella would be better than a tin hat!

The Blackout

If German pilots saw lights, they would know where to drop their bombs. So the government told people not to use lights at night. This was called the blackout.

People had to buy thick, dark curtains, or stick brown paper over their windows. Some factory windows were painted black. People could then work inside with the lights on.

White stripes were painted on pavement kerbs and lamp-posts to help people find their way in the dark. People were allowed to use torches covered with tissue paper.

▶ Cows were painted with white stripes so drivers could see them.

UNTIL YOUR EYES
GET USED TO
THE DARKNESS,
TAKE IT EASY

LOOK OUT IN THE BLACKOUT

◀ This poster warned people to be careful in the blackout.

▼ The government warned people to take care crossing the road.

HE THOUGHT HE COULD JUST DO IT

It wasn't far—just a few yards across the road. He wanted to catch the 'bus home, so he took a chance and ran for it. Death happened to get in his way. It was nothing very unusual; literally hundreds of people are killed or injured in the black-out every week. Nearly 1,200 road deaths in December alone. Remember the new speed limit cannot alter the fact that you can see the car before the driver can see you. How often do you hurry and 'just' do it'? Will the luck hold?

Remember these   1 When you first come out into the black-out, stand still for a minute to get your eyes used to the darkness.
Your Safety Rules 2 Look both ways before stepping off the pavement.
3 Where there are traffic lights, always cross by them. It is worth going out of your way to do this.
4 Throw the light of your torch down on to the ground, so that you do not dazzle drivers.

LOOK OUT IN THE BLACK-OUT!

Getting around in the blackout was very dangerous. The street lights were turned off and no car headlights were allowed. Many people were killed in car accidents. So it was agreed that people could use car headlights with hoods over them.

The First Air Raid

Many months passed before any bombing started. Then, on 7 September 1940, German bombers made their first big daylight raid. The skies were filled with 350 bombers and 650 fighter planes.

The targets for the bombs were the docks in London. Planes flew in, circled round and dropped their bombs on the docks. As they flew off, more planes attacked.

▼ Firemen try to put out fires started by the German bombs.

◀ Many fires were started in the docks.

Fire and smoke

Soon a great cloud of smoke could be seen from miles away. All the fire engines in London raced to the docks, clanging their bells loudly.

One person wrote: 'The cloud grew to such a size that we gasped; there could not ever in history have been so gigantic a fire.'

By evening, the fire lit up the sky. The bombing continued all through the night.

◀ This German bomber was known as a 'flying pencil'.

London in the Blitz

The day of the first air raid was called Black Saturday. Many people were badly hurt, and 448 people were killed. Bombs destroyed hundreds of homes. The streets were filled with bricks, dust, smoke and the smell of bombs.

A child described the bombs falling: 'I felt the earth juddering under me ... it seemed as if the whole air was falling apart.'

▼ A warden searches a bombed house.

London was bombed for fifty-seven nights in a row. This was called the Blitz.

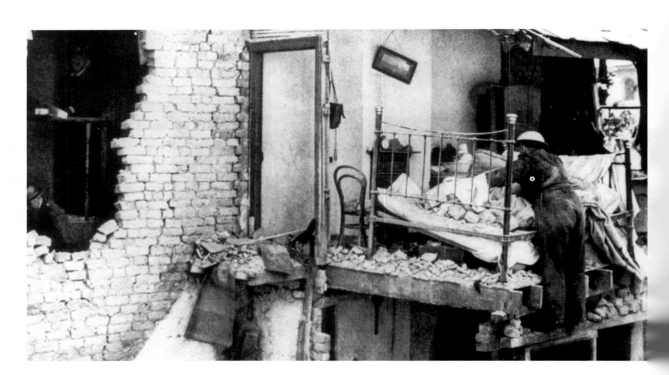

More anti-aircraft guns were brought in to defend London. People cheered as the guns started to fire at the German planes. Powerful searchlights helped the gunners to see the planes.

Huge balloons, called barrage balloons, were floated above London. They forced the bombers to stay high up in the sky. This made it hard for them to hit their targets.

▼ Soldiers look for German bomber planes with a searchlight.

▼ The Home Guard practise firing an anti-aircraft gun.

Underground Shelters

▲ People buying food in the Underground.

As the bombing continued, people became tired. It was hard to get any sleep. Some people decided to sleep down in the London Underground. They felt safe in the tunnels.

The government tried to stop people sleeping in the Underground stations. But people were determined. A writer described how a crowd forced their way into one station: 'A great yell went up and the gates were opened.'

▶ Families slept in the Underground tunnels and on the platforms.

At some stations, people bought tickets then refused to leave. They queued up for a space to sleep. Children ran along the platform under the legs of adults, and saved a space for their family.

Up to 60,000 people sheltered in seventy-nine Underground stations. With so many people crowded into the Underground, it was uncomfortable and smelly.

But things got better. Volunteers gave out buns and drinks. Many children thought that sleeping in the Underground was an exciting game.

▲ A bus stuck in a bomb crater. The bomb destroyed an Underground station. Many people who were sheltering there were killed.

Bomb Damage

Daylight bombing raids went on. The Germans wanted the RAF to attack their bomber planes. They could then bring in their fighters to shoot down the RAF planes. Hitler also hoped the raids would terrify the British people.

On one night, 900 fires were reported. Railways and roads were destroyed. People also had no gas, electricity or water because of bomb damage.

▼ A building collapses after being bombed.

HOLDING THE LINE!

▲ A cartoon of Winston Churchill, the British prime minister. It shows him as a brave bulldog.

Heavy "Stirling" bombers raid the Nazi Baltic port of Lübeck and leave the docks ablaze

BACK THEM UP!

▲ A poster showing British planes bombing German ships.

No surrender

The bombing was not as bad as people had expected. They refused to give in despite the damage.

Meanwhile, the RAF was bombing cities in Germany. People there felt the same way as the British people. They were angry and frightened, but they would not give in.

Sirens and Shelters

A siren went off when a bombing raid started. It made a wailing noise. Some people called it Moaning Minnie.

People heard many other noises. Some bombs whistled. Others sounded like sheets being torn. Firebombs clattered on roofs. Anti-aircraft guns thudded. When a house blew up, there was a loud crash.

▲ Wardens used a rattle like this to warn people of danger.

▶ A warden inspects an air-raid shelter.

Air-raid shelters

Air-raid wardens got to know where people sheltered during a raid. Some people stayed at home, in the cellar or under the stairs. Some stayed in bed. If a bomb hit a house, the wardens knew where to start digging to get people out.

Many people went to public shelters. Some shelters were badly built and they did not have proper toilets. No one had expected raids to last for so many hours. As people spent more time in shelters, they were made more comfortable.

▲ Garden shelters were called Anderson shelters. This one kept a family safe when their house was bombed.

Coventry is Bombed

Hitler decided to start bombing the British cities where aeroplanes, tanks and guns were made. On the night of 14 November 1940, the Germans bombed Coventry. The pilots could see the city clearly in the bright moonlight.

The centre of the city was burned to the ground. Coventry Cathedral was ruined.

▼ A notice warned people to boil drinking water, because bombs had damaged drains.

CITY OF COVENTRY

PREVENTION of TYPHOID FEVER

In view of present damage to DRAINAGE communications in the City, special precautions against Typhoid Fever are advised

BOIL ALL DRINKING WATER

▼ This is how the centre of Coventry looked after it was bombed.

A CHAIN OF BUCKETS

THE STIRRUP HAND PUMP

LIGHT TRAILER FIRE-PUMP

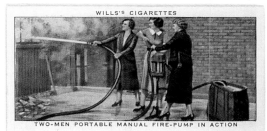

TWO-MEN PORTABLE MANUAL FIRE-PUMP IN ACTION

◄ The people of Coventry used many different ways to put out fires.

▼ Winston Churchill, the prime minister of Britain.

Twenty-one factories in Coventry were destroyed. There were no buses or trains. The shops were closed. Telephones did not work. There was no water. People were in a daze.

Winston Churchill knew the Germans would bomb Coventry, because the German secret code had been broken. But he did not want the Germans to know this, so people were not sent out of the city. The bombing raid killed 568 people.

Bombing the Cities

After Coventry, the Germans bombed cities all over Britain. Many people were injured. Extra beds were put in hospital corridors.

Southampton was so badly damaged that fires were still burning two days after the bombing. Bombs did so much damage that people did not recognize their own streets.

▲ Bombed houses were left empty. If people were caught stealing from them, they could be executed.

▶ This map shows the cities that were bombed in Britain. The German air force was called the Luftwaffe.

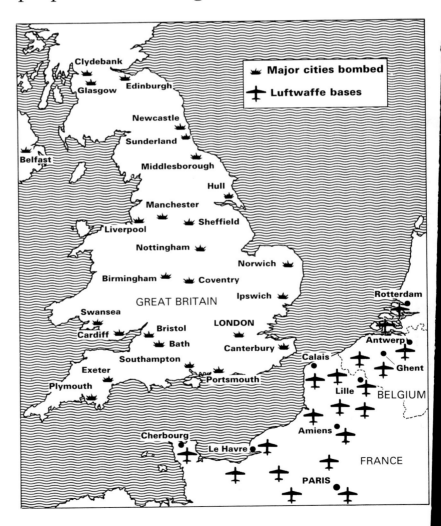

Morrison shelters

A new sort of shelter was made, called a Morrison shelter. It was a big metal table with wire mesh along the sides.

Morrison shelters were used inside people's houses. They kept people safe from flying glass and bricks, even when their houses collapsed.

One man described what it was like sitting under a Morrison shelter when his house was bombed: 'I saw the walls of the room crumbling and tumbling towards us ... and then – I could scarce believe it – the night sky! Our house had completely vanished!'

▲ This family is using their Morrison shelter as a table-tennis table.

London on Fire

Many German planes dropped firebombs which could set light to buildings. The worst night of firebombing for London was 29 December 1940.

The bombers flew in, and began dropping bunches of firebombs. It was a Sunday and all the offices in London were locked. Firemen could not get into the locked buildings to put out each fire as it started. Soon the City of London was ablaze.

▼ St Paul's Cathedral was surrounded by smoke on the night of the firebombing.

▲ A poster telling people to watch out for fires.

▲ St Paul's Cathedral after the fire. Somehow, the cathedral survived.

Water in the River Thames was very low, and there were no emergency tanks of water. The firemen could not get enough water to put out the huge fires.

St Paul's Cathedral was surrounded by flames. People were amazed to see it still standing when the fires were finally put out. After this night, the government ordered people to watch out for fires.

The Horror of Fire

Fire caused terrible damage in many cities. When the docks in London were bombed, big stores of wood caught light. Firemen travelled from other cities to help fight the huge fire.

The fire in the docks was so hot that boats on the other side of the river had their paint scorched.

▼ Firemen putting out a fire in London.

◄ The German city of Cologne was bombed by planes from Britain and the USA.

At Clydebank in Scotland, a sugar store was bombed. The melted sugar flowed out of the store in a gluey, fiery river. It looked like the lava from a volcano. When it cooled down, the sugar was scooped up and cleaned. People could not afford to waste it because they had so little food.

Bombing Germany

British and American planes bombed German cities just as heavily. The whole of the city of Dresden was destroyed. Thousands of people were burnt to death.

▲ The story of the bombing of Dresden was on the front page of newspapers.

— Rockets and Flying Bombs —

After May 1941, the Germans needed their bombers to fight against Russia. The Blitz was over.

But in 1944, Germany attacked Britain with new weapons launched from France. First, they launched flying bombs called V-1s. Later, they fired huge rockets called V-2s, which did even more damage.

▶ A V-1 flying bomb, which people in Britain called a 'doodlebug'.

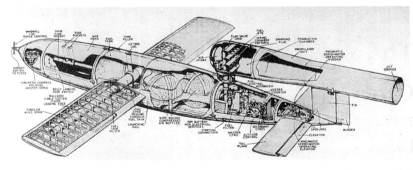

▼ A V-2 rocket.

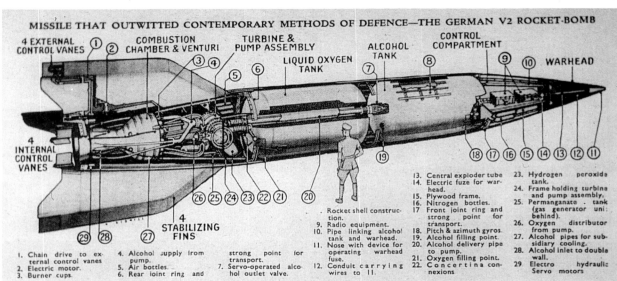

MISSILE THAT OUTWITTED CONTEMPORARY METHODS OF DEFENCE—THE GERMAN V2 ROCKET-BOMB

1. Chain drive to external control vanes.
2. Electric motor.
3. Burner cups.
4. Alcohol supply from pump.
5. Air bottles.
6. Rear joint ring and strong point for transport.
7. Servo-operated alcohol outlet valve.
8. Rocket shell construction.
9. Radio equipment.
10. Pipe linking alcohol tank and warhead.
11. Nose with device for operating warhead fuse.
12. Conduit carrying wires to 11.
13. Central exploder tube
14. Electric fuze for warhead.
15. Plywood frame.
16. Nitrogen bottles.
17. Front joint ring and strong point for transport.
18. Pitch & azimuth gyros.
19. Alcohol filling point.
20. Alcohol delivery pipe to pump.
21. Oxygen filling point.
22. Concertina connexions.
23. Hydrogen peroxide tank.
24. Frame holding turbine and pump assembly.
25. Permanganate tank (gas generator unit behind).
26. Oxygen distributor from pump.
27. Alcohol pipes for subsidiary cooling.
28. Alcohol inlet to double wall.
29. Electro hydraulic Servo motors

The end of the war

Germany suffered more damage from air raids than Britain did. Both countries bombed factories at the beginning of the war. Then they bombed cities where they knew many people would be killed. But bombing did not make people want to surrender or give up.

The British and the Americans joined up with the Russians to defeat Hitler. In May 1945 the war ended in Europe. Germany was defeated.

▲ A German city after the war. You can see how much damage bombs have caused.

Glossary

air raids Bombing attacks made by enemy aeroplanes.

anti-aircraft guns Guns used for firing at enemy aeroplanes.

barrage balloons Large balloons with ropes hanging from them, which are used to stop planes flying low.

bomb crater A hole in the ground made by an exploding bomb.

firebombs Bombs which start fires when they explode.

Home Guard Part-time soldiers who helped defend Britain from the Germans.

juddering Shaking.

lava The hot liquid which flows from a volcano.

searchlights Very big lights, which helped gunners to see enemy planes in the dark.

siren A machine that makes a loud noise as a warning.

Underground The railway which travels under the ground in London.

Projects

1 Ask your family and neighbours if they remember the Blitz. These are some questions you can ask them:

- Where did you live?
- What sort of shelter did you use?
- What sounds can you remember?

2 Imagine that it is 1940. An air raid is starting. You have to get to the shelter. What would you take with you? Look for clues in the pictures in this book.

Books to Read

Children of the Blitz by Robert Westall (Piccolo, 1995)

Evidence from the Home Front by Ruth Currie & Sheila Livingstone (Thomas Nelson & Sons, 1990)

Home in the Blitz by Marilyn Tolhurst (A & C Black, 1996)

Johnnie's Blitz by Bernard Ashley (Viking, 1995)

Places to Visit

Britain at War Experience, 64 Tooley Street, London. Tel: 0171 378 1147
Here, you can try on tin helmets, gas masks and uniforms.

Eden Camp, Malton, North Yorkshire. Tel: 01653 697777
This museum tells you about everyday life during World War II.

The Imperial War Museum, London. Tel: 0171 416 5313
This museum has displays showing you what life was like in the Blitz.

Use this book for teaching literacy

This book can help you in the literacy hour in the following ways:

- ✓ Children can use the contents page, page numbers, headings, captions and index to locate a particular piece of information.
- ✓ Posters, advertisements and newspaper headlines are good examples of the different styles of writing needed for Year 4 literacy teaching.
- ✓ Children can use the glossary to reinforce their alphabetic knowledge and extend their vocabulary.
- ✓ They can compare this book with fictional stories about the Blitz to show how similar information can be presented in different ways.

Index

Numbers in **bold** refer
to pictures and captions.